10 Writing Lessons for the Overhead

BY LOLA SCHAEFER

SCHOLASTIC
PROFESSIONAL BOOKS

NEW YORK • TORONTO • LONDON • AUCKLAND • SYDNEY
MEXICO CITY • NEW DELHI • HONG KONG • BUENOS AIRES

To the dedicated teachers of student writers—

keep demonstrating and encouraging

A C K N O W L E D G M E N T S

Thank you, Connie, for walking this path with me.

My sincere appreciation to my editors,
Wendy Murray and Joanna Davis-Swing,
who listen to each new idea with enthusiasm
and offer continued support through the
creative process.

Scholastic Inc. grants teachers permission to photocopy the pattern pages from this book for classroom use. No other part of this publication may be reproduced in whole or in part, or stored in a retrieval system, or transmitted in any form or by any means, electronic, mechanical, photocopying, recording, or otherwise, without written permission of the publisher. For information regarding permission, write to Scholastic Inc., 557 Broadway, New York, NY 10012.

Cover photograph by Clint Keller
Cover design by James Sarfati
Interior photographs: Pages 6, 18, 31, 47, and 72 by Clint Keller;
Pages 12 and 54 by Vicki Kasala; Pages 24 and 39 by Michael C. York; Page 61 by Joan Beard.
Interior design by Kathy Massaro

ISBN 0-439-30940-9
Copyright © 2002 by Lola Schaefer
All rights reserved.
Printed in U.S.A.

8 9 10   40   09 08 07 06 05

CONTENTS

Introduction

The Power of Writing Samples

Teachers are always searching for new ways to help students improve their writing. While teaching grades two to seven, I often read aloud and then referred to examples of elements of good writing in published works. In addition, I would display paragraphs and stories written by previous students on the overhead projector to spark discussions of meaning, vocabulary, organization, voice, or other craft elements. Students could readily identify these features in another writer's work. Later, they would patiently try to add those craft elements to their writing.

During the past four years I have been working as a writing consultant in elementary and middle schools. As my instruction became more defined, I wrote overhead samples that pinpointed specific elements of writing. These samples strengthened my mini-lessons and helped students improve the quality of their pieces. Through experimentation, I developed a technique that quickly makes students aware of key writing elements. I generate two to four writing samples (all on the same topic) and place them on the overhead projector, one at a time, in no specific order. Instead of stating my opinion of each piece, I ask questions that guide students to recognize the strengths or weaknesses of each sample.

These are not masterpieces. One is always poorly written. I have learned that students need to see a range of pieces from poor to excellent to improve their own writing. In fact, the poorly written example is a necessity. Students scorn its boring cadence, lack of detail, or robot-like voice and vow never to write like that. They laugh at the bland vocabulary of *nice, went,* and *pretty* and call out words or similes that would describe, or *show*, instead of *tell.* I've come to know that it's the unimaginative piece, the telling piece, that helps push young writers in the right direction.

Conversely, they need to see the well-crafted pieces, too. They relish details that make them laugh or wonder. Students recognize specific vocabulary and ask questions about these words, adding them to their own working vocabularies. They become savvy about what works in a particular piece of writing. The results of using a broad spectrum of samples are significant. I've seen tremendous growth in the quality of first drafts and revision comments in the classrooms where I have been using these demonstration pieces.

How to Use the Samples in This Book

The writing sample sets and lessons in this book are not intended to replace discussions centered around published writing, peer critiques, or teacher conferences. Instead, use a set of pieces as an extended mini-lesson when you sense that your students need more specific help in learning one particular element of writing. You can use them to:

1. Introduce a new craft element to your students

2. Reinforce efforts you've seen your students make

3. Nudge students into revision with one element in mind

I have found the greatest results when reusing the same samples within a short time frame. For instance, if I'm working with third graders on voice, I might introduce voice with the entire set and guide students to discover which sample(s) have a true writer's voice. A few days later when students are moving into peer conferences and revision, I'll place those examples of voice on the overhead projector again. I'll lead them through a discussion so they can again identify the phrases and dialogue that add voice to that writing. Now that students are emotionally involved in their own pieces, they are more likely to re-examine their writing with a critical eye to find opportunities where they can improve the voice.

The anonymity of the pieces ensures a safe, comfortable environment for discussion. Students aren't worried that their writing, with or without name, will suddenly appear on the overhead projector. These samples are simply working models, with no personal consequences of fame or shame for anyone in the classroom.

I recommend using one set of samples for at least two weeks before introducing another element of writing. We want upper-grade students to identify, apply, practice, and recognize each writing element before adding another. After you see the power of these kinds of pieces, you can generate additional examples for your students.

We teach the tools of writing so students will be able to communicate more effectively. Our main goal always remains to provide the strategies and skills that enable every student to express his or her thoughts and ideas. Use these samples to enhance your students' understanding of the craft of writing. Then step back and encourage them to take risks and write boldly about what they know and feel.

Meaning

THE QUESTION TO EXPLORE

Does the Writing Make Sense?

When writing, an author rushes to get his ideas on paper. The meaning is clear in the writer's mind. He knows what he wants to say. The writer tries to record everything as he thinks of it. But sometimes the meaning on paper isn't as clear as the meaning in his head. There can be too many ideas, a lack of order or sequence, or no real structure to guide the reader. Since meaning is essential to all forms of communication, it's the first element of craft I invite students to identify and evaluate.

Introducing the Craft Element: Meaning

Before you show and discuss the overhead transparencies on *Meaning*, have the following discussion with your students.

Teacher: Writers share ideas, thoughts, stories, memories, images, or information with an audience. It is important that the reader understands what the writer has written. Otherwise, the writer's meaning is lost. A writer can only communicate with others if his or her writing can be easily understood.

Please, listen carefully to these sentences:

> **It started up again. The roar of the engines, the clank of the wheels, and the squeal of the whistles kept me awake late into the night.**

Now, tell me everything that you understand from what I said.

Responses will vary. One child might say that this person could not sleep because of the noises. Another may say that the writer heard the noises earlier, too. Someone else might say that the author sounds upset or frustrated.

Teacher: What are you talking about? What is making this noise?

Students might guess what it is: a car, a big machine, a train, an airplane—but finally someone will say, we don't know for sure.

Teacher: Why can't you tell me what is making this noise? Did this author do a good job of telling you everything you needed to know to make sense of those sentences?

Students: No!

Teacher: Please, listen to these sentences:

> **The trains started moving again. The roar of the engines, the clank of the wheels, and the squeal of the whistles kept me awake late into the night.**

Now tell me everything you understood from what I said.

Students: The noise of trains was keeping the writer up late. The trains started moving again. Their engines, wheels, and whistles were the noises.

Teacher: Which set of sentences made the more sense? Which set was more easily understood?

Students: The second set.

Teacher: Why?

Students: Because we knew what was making the noise. We knew how it was making noise. We knew that the noise was keeping the author awake. The first one didn't tell us everything. This one did.

Teacher: Yes. An audience likes to get all the information to be able to understand what the author is writing. This year we want to be able to check that our writing carries meaning. We want to share the meaning in our heads with our audiences. Let's look at some writing and see if the meaning is clear.

Discussing the Craft Element: Meaning

Place sample #2 of the *Meaning* transparency on the overhead projector. Cover the other two writing samples while you and your students examine #2. Read it out loud with expression, then ask these questions:

- Do you understand everything that the author has written?
- Are there any words or ideas that seem confusing?
- Does it all make sense to you?
- Does this writing carry meaning?

Repeat this process for each of the samples on the transparency, continuing to cover samples not in use. If one piece has obvious lapses in meaning and the students are not identifying those passages, you may want to read each sentence independently again and ask one or two of these questions after each one. After all samples have been read and evaluated ask the students: *Which sample is the easiest to understand? Why?*

After all samples have been viewed and discussed, it is sometimes helpful to put all three pieces on the overhead projector and compare strengths and weaknesses.

Discussion Points

If students cannot tell you why they think sample #3 is the strongest piece in meaning, ask these questions:

- How did the author first tell us the topic of the paragraph?
- What kinds of information did we learn in the first sentence?
- Which specific pieces of vocabulary added meaning to the story?
- Which word(s) in each sentence help us keep the meaning clear?

Clarify Meaning: Tips for Teachers and Students

1. The title helps establish meaning.

2. The lead sentence tells exactly what the paragraph is about.

   SAMPLE 2: Last night, my family got a new dog.

3. Specific vocabulary adds meaning.

   SAMPLE 3: German shepherd, Woodland Kennel, and **licked my hand** all give more information to the reader.

4. Clear, identifiable subjects in all sentences establish meaning.

   Mom and Dad (**SAMPLE 3**) is a more specific subject than **we** without an antecedent (**SAMPLE 1**).

ACTION LIST FOR STUDENTS

What Can We Do to Clarify Meaning?

▲ ▲ ▲ ▲ ▲

1. Check that your title leads the audience into the piece.

2. Read your piece out loud and ask, "Does this writing make sense?"

3. Read your piece to friends and ask if your writing makes sense.

4. Have friends circle with colored pencil any places where the meaning is confusing so you can rewrite those passages.

①

Last night we got him. He was my favorite one at the kennel. Other dogs had mean eyes. Some dogs growled. But my dog came and licked me. It was fun. I liked it. We never get things right away. It usually takes us a long time to make up our minds. I knew we wouldn't get this dog right away. We did! We went to the grocery store. We bought him some things he would need. He's at our house now and I'm happy.

A New Dog

②

Last night, my family got a new dog. It was my favorite at the dog kennel. Some had mean-looking eyes. Others growled. But this dog came right up to me and started to lick. I didn't think we would get it then. I thought we would have to go to a lot of other places. I was surprised. We did get it. We stopped and got a collar and a food bowl. It is our dog now and I am glad.

Our New Dog

Last night, my family and I got a new German Shepherd puppy. It was the friendliest dog at Woodland Kennel. Some dogs had mean-looking eyes. Other dogs growled when we walked up to them. One dog, Rascal, ran to me and licked my hand like it was a Popsicle™ on a hot day. I knew right away that he was my favorite. Mom and Dad surprised me! Instead of visiting the other three kennels on our list, they immediately bought Rascal and we took him with us. We stopped at the grocery store and bought his first dog collar and food bowl. I think Rascal and I are going to be good friends.

MINI 2 LESSON

FOCUS

THE QUESTION TO EXPLORE

Does the Writing Stay on One Topic?

To maintain focus, a writer stays on one topic throughout a piece of writing. Focus is an essential element of strong writing that is fairly simple to teach. A brief plan, such as a story plan, a web, a simple outline, or another graphic organizer can help many writers maintain their focus throughout a story, poem, or informational piece. If an author organizes her thoughts before writing, it helps her develop the topic and not stray from the intended purpose and audience.

Introducing the Craft Element: Focus

Begin your mini-lesson on focus like this:

Teacher: Does anyone know what the focus control does for your TV or computer monitor?

Student: It makes the picture clear. It takes away the fuzzy parts.

Teacher: Exactly. Maintaining a focus in writing does the same thing. It keeps the purpose of the writing clear. If you have focus in your writing, you will not allow extra information to "fuzz" your meaning. When we focus, we concentrate. Our writing concentrates on one topic and purpose.

Let's look at three written samples and discover which one is most focused and why.

Discussing the Craft Element: Focus

Place sample #2 of the *Focus* transparencies on the overhead projector. Read it out loud with expression. Afterward, ask these questions:

❋ Do you understand what the author has written?

❋ Does it make sense?

Since these samples are designed to show only differences in focus, the meaning should be clear. Students will tell you that they understand what the author is saying, even in the sample that is poorly focused. Respond enthusiastically. *Good, I'm glad to know that the meaning is strong in this piece. The author has achieved one of her goals.* Continue with these questions:

❋ What topic or subject has the author written about?

❋ Does everything in this piece stay on that topic?

❋ Are there any phrases or sentences that lose that focus?

❋ Are there any words that need to be removed from this piece?

If the students seem to miss obvious errors in focus, you may decide to read the piece again, one sentence at a time. After each sentence ask one or two focus questions from the above list. Also, you may want to highlight the words, phrases, or sentences that students identify as "off the focus." In another color, highlight the words, phrases, or sentences that are focused. Visual learners will respond well to this color identification. Repeat the procedure for each sample.

After you have read and discussed each sample ask the students:

❋ Which piece is the most focused?

❋ What did this author do that made this writing more focused than the other two?

Stay Focused!

Learning How to Cook

My dad is teaching me how to cook. Every night we make dinner together. So far we have made toasted cheese sandwiches, tuna casserole, potato soup, and tacos. Cooking is harder work than it looks. It takes time to get everything ready. All ingredients must be measured correctly. Then, you need to wait while it cooks. My favorite dinners were the toasted cheese sandwiches and the tacos because we didn't have to wait long. But sometimes the wait is good because while you smell the food, you get hungrier and hungrier. That makes the food taste even better!

① All text remains on the focus in this piece.

Learning How to Cook

My dad is teaching me how to cook. Every night we make dinner together while our neighbors go out to eat. Cooking is harder work than it looks. It takes time to get everything ready. All ingredients must be measured correctly. Sometimes I spill food on the floor and our cat comes over and smells it. She'll eat it if it's something good like tuna, milk, or cheese. Otherwise, she just steps in it and walks away. Then, you need to wait while it cooks. My favorite dinners were the toasted cheese sandwiches and the tacos because we didn't have to wait long. But sometimes the wait is good because while you smell the food, you get hungrier and hungrier. That makes the food taste even better!

 These words stray from the focus.

Learning How to Cook

My dad is teaching me how to cook. Every night we make dinner together. After that I have to do my homework and Dad watches the news on TV. He makes me sit in another room to do my homework so the TV doesn't bother me. But I'd rather be with him than by myself. So far my favorite dinners were toasted cheese sandwiches and tacos because we didn't have to wait long to eat. But sometimes the wait is good. You get hungrier and hungrier while you smell the food cooking. The wait makes it taste even better when I eat it!

 These words stray from the focus.

Discussion Points

If students cannot tell you why sample #1 is more focused, ask these questions while showing that piece on the overhead projector:

❄ What was the author's topic or subject for this paragraph?

❄ When did we first know that this was the author's topic?

❄ What different aspects of cooking and food did the author explain?

❄ Does every sentence have something to do with cooking or food?

Clarify Focus: Tips for Teachers and Students

1. The title gives a clue to the focus.

Samples are titled "Learning How to Cook"; all are about the author learning to cook with dad.

2. Each sentence relates to the focus stated in the topic sentence(s).

In **SAMPLE 1**, the focus is stated in the first sentence: **My dad is teaching me how to cook.** The author goes on to explain when they cook, what they have cooked, some of the difficulties in cooking, favorite dinners, and how a long wait can enhance the flavor of food.

ACTION LIST FOR STUDENTS

What Can We Do to Remain Focused?

▲ ▲ ▲ ▲ ▲

1. Create a brief plan or use a graphic organizer before writing.

2. Identify the topic or subject that is the focus of your writing.

3. Examine each sentence and ask, "Does the writing stay on one topic?"

4. Ask a friend to read your draft and check if all sentences stay on topic.

5. Ask a friend to circle any passages that do not stay on focus.

Learning How to Cook

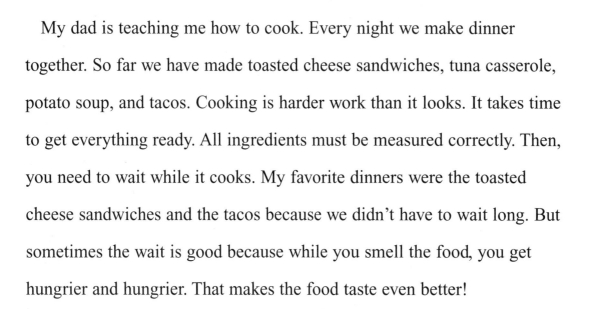

My dad is teaching me how to cook. Every night we make dinner together. So far we have made toasted cheese sandwiches, tuna casserole, potato soup, and tacos. Cooking is harder work than it looks. It takes time to get everything ready. All ingredients must be measured correctly. Then, you need to wait while it cooks. My favorite dinners were the toasted cheese sandwiches and the tacos because we didn't have to wait long. But sometimes the wait is good because while you smell the food, you get hungrier and hungrier. That makes the food taste even better!

Learning How to Cook

My dad is teaching me how to cook. Every night we make dinner together while our neighbors go out to eat. Cooking is harder work than it looks. It takes time to get everything ready. All ingredients must be measured correctly. Sometimes I spill food on the floor and our cat comes over and smells it. She'll eat it if it's something good like tuna, milk, or cheese. Otherwise, she just steps in it and walks away. Then, you need to wait while it cooks. My favorite dinners were the toasted cheese sandwiches and the tacos because we didn't have to wait long. But sometimes the wait is good because while you smell the food, you get hungrier and hungrier. That makes the food taste even better!

10 Writing Lessons for the Overhead   Scholastic Professional Books

Learning How to Cook

My dad is teaching me how to cook. Every night we make dinner together. After that I have to do my homework and Dad watches the news on TV. He makes me sit in another room to do my homework so the TV doesn't bother me. But I'd rather be with him than by myself. So far my favorite dinners were toasted cheese sandwiches and tacos because we didn't have to wait long to eat. But sometimes the wait is good. You get hungrier and hungrier while you smell the food cooking. The wait makes it taste even better when I eat it!

Vocabulary

Do the Words Paint a Specific Picture?

Specific vocabulary adds meaning and interest to a piece of writing. The more precise the language, the more distinct the images writers can offer their audience. Of all the elements of strong writing, vocabulary is the one that most students enjoy identifying and improving. They immediately see the value in specific word choice and take pride in expanding their working vocabularies.

Introducing the Craft Element: Vocabulary

Begin your mini-lesson on vocabulary like this:

Teacher: Please, shut your eyes and think of what you see when I say the word *insect*. What did you see in your mind?

Answers will vary from mosquito to ant to fly to beetle, etc.

Teacher: Please, shut your eyes again and think of what you see when I say *monarch butterfly*. What did you see in your mind?

Most answers will specifically describe the shape and colors of a monarch.

Teacher: Which vocabulary was more specific? Which term painted a more detailed picture in your mind? *Insect*? Or *monarch butterfly*?

You may opt to offer more specific examples of this type of vocabulary difference. Some other sets of words you might choose to use are: *kid* and *toddler*, *bushes* and *hedge*, *sat* and *lounged*; *music* and *rap*; *hair* and *crewcut*; *book* and *comic book*; *cried* and *whimpered*; *ate* and *gulped*; and *kept* and *treasured*.

The purpose of this short exercise is to help students discover that precise vocabulary calls up a specific image in the mind of the reader. Students quickly recognize that general terms are just that—vague. They leave readers guessing at the exact meaning of the author. As writers, we want to guarantee our audiences specific images and meaning. Exact word choice is another way to perfect meaning.

Follow-up

A great follow-up that reinforces this idea is inviting students to compare sentences on the same topic, one written in vague terms, the other with precise vocabulary. Let the students decide which sentence offers the audience an exact image.

Teacher: Please, shut your eyes and listen to this sentence:

The girl saw her big dog with her cat.

Now, tell me what you saw in your head when I said that sentence.

Give several students an opportunity to describe their mental images. While they are reporting, ask them questions: *Was the dog white? Black? Where was the girl? How old was she?* Make a point of discovering that there were many images for the same sentence.

Teacher: Please, shut your eyes again and listen to another sentence:

> **Seven-year-old Amanda stared as her St. Bernard cuddled with her calico kitten on the kitchen linoleum.**

Again, ask a few students to describe their mental images. Compare sentences.

Teacher: Which of these two sentences paints a more specific picture in your mind? Which word is more specific? *Amanda* or *girl*? *Dog* or *St. Bernard*? *Cat* or *kitten*? An author always tries to select words that say exactly what she wants to say.

Discussing the Craft Element: Vocabulary

Place sample #2 of the *Vocabulary* transparency on the overhead projector. Read it out loud to the students with expression. Ask these questions:

※ Do you understand what the author has written?

※ Does it make sense?

Since these pieces are designed to show only the differences in weak and strong vocabulary, students will tell you that they can understand the writing and it does make sense. Next ask:

※ Is this piece focused?

※ Does all the writing remain on one topic or subject?

Again, students will answer yes. Continue with these questions:

※ Do these words paint a specific picture in your mind?

※ Are there any words that are too general? (**SAMPLE 1: kids, put them into, went, moving, big stuff, some land, went in and out, looked at all the stuff**)

※ What do these words do for the writing?

※ Which words are specific? (**SAMPLE 2: Cammi and Jeff, canoe, rocked, paddles, shore, rocked, dipped, river water, drifted, maneuvering, knotted trees, heron, swooped, mud flat, sunbathed, sandbar, fawn, steady rhythm, panoramic view; SAMPLE 1: canoe, rocked, paddles, downstream, turtles, baby deer**)

※ Let's circle these words and see how many precise vocabulary words the author used in this paragraph.

Repeat the process outlined above for the other piece. Students will tell you that #1 is boring. I've never used that word, but kids always seem to apply it to the piece with bland vocabulary. After both samples have been viewed and discussed, it is sometimes helpful to put both pieces on the overhead projector at the same time and compare strengths and weaknesses.

Discussion Points

If students cannot tell why piece #2 is stronger, ask these questions:

❋ Which piece uses the most specific vocabulary?

❋ Does this word make the writing more interesting? How?

❋ Does this word add more meaning?

❋ Which words in sample #2 are stronger than in sample #1?

Students will list many examples of specific vocabulary from sample #2. They enjoy this exercise when they can see both samples at the same time and explain why one word is stronger than another.

Clarify Vocabulary Use: Tips for Teachers and Students

1. Specific vocabulary paints a clear picture in the reader's mind.

   The names **Cammi** and **Jeff** are more specific than **two kids**.
   Dipped is more specific than **put them in**.
   Friends is more specific than **kids**.
   Maneuvering is more specific than **moving**.

2. Specific vocabulary adds meaning by giving the reader more detail.

   SAMPLE 2: A heron swooped near them and landed on a mud flat gives the reader the name of the exact bird, describes how it flew, and specifies the place it landed.

What Can We Do to Use More Specific Vocabulary?

▲ ▲ ▲ ▲ ▲

1. Use a student dictionary or thesaurus to find more specific language.

2. Make a list of words that don't paint precise pictures and avoid their use. Words to begin the list could be *nice, stuff, a lot, went, pretty, then,* or *moved.*

3. Read one sentence at a time from your writing and ask, "Are the words specific?"

4. Set a goal to use four to six pieces of specific vocabulary in all your writing.

5. Ask friends to read your writing and circle with colored pencil two to three weak and general words that can be improved.

The Canoe Trip

The two kids pushed off. Their canoe rocked when they picked up their paddles and put them into the water. The kids went downstream, moving their canoe around big stuff. A bird flew down near them and stood on some land. Turtles sat on broken branches. When their canoe slowed up, they saw a baby deer swimming to land. The kids' paddles went in and out of the water together. They didn't talk. Instead, they looked at all the stuff around them.

The Canoe Trip

Cammi and Jeff pushed away from shore. Their canoe rocked as they picked up their paddles and dipped them into the river water. The friends drifted downstream, maneuvering around rocks and knotted trees. A heron swooped near them and landed on a mud flat. Turtles sun-bathed on fallen branches. When their canoe slowed near a sandbar, they watched a fawn swim to shore. Cammi and Jeff's paddles fell into a steady rhythm. No one spoke. Instead, they enjoyed the panoramic view.

Show, Don't Tell

Does the Writing Show What's Happening?

All writers hear the phrase *show, don't tell* repeatedly in writing class. Show the audience what was said, how it was said, how someone moved, what they saw. Take the audience to the scene—make it come alive for them. I always explain that *show* is an immediate way of pulling the audience into the writing. *Tell* keeps the audience at arm's length. It sends the message: Stay away! Don't get involved. Just skim the surface.

Introducing the Craft Element: Show

Begin your mini-lesson on show, don't tell like this:

Teacher: I'd like you to shut your eyes and listen to this sentence:

Derek was very frustrated as he stood at home plate.

Now, show me through a series of actions what you saw in your mind.

This requires kids to get up out of their seats and move around. Actions will vary considerably.

Teacher: Please, shut your eyes again and listen to this sentence:

Derek clenched his teeth, pulled back his bat, and vowed, "I will keep my eyes on this next ball and hit it!"

Again, show me what you saw in your mind.

Most students will repeat the actions word for word in their mini-dramas.

Teacher: Which sentence showed you Derek's frustration? Which sentence offered the best meaning? Which sentence painted the clearest image in your mind?

Writers try to *show* the action of the character, rather than just *tell* about it. When a writer shows her audience what is happening, she may:

- Describe the character's actions rather than just say how she feels
- Use active verbs
- Describe a specific setting
- Use similes to create images
- Use dialogue
- Show what the character is thinking
- Use some of the five senses to paint a picture of what is happening

As an extension, you can give your students these examples to draw, describe, or act out.

Therese was frightened.	**Therese gasped for air as she struggled to stay above the waves.**
Rebel was a good dog.	**Rebel obediently sat at his master's side until a raised hand commanded him to retrieve the ball.**
The lightning flashed all over.	**Jagged bolts of lightning criss-crossed the sky in a maze of light.**

Students Show

For more quick practice on *Show, Don't Tell* give your students a general (tell) sentence and ask them to change it to *show*. The variety of responses is entertaining and informative. Here are a few practice sentences:

❋ **A star moved fast across the sky.**

❋ **She looked down and cried.**

❋ **His paper airplane flew through the room.**

❋ **He was worried about the test.**

Discussing the Craft Element: Show, Don't Tell

Place a sample from the *Show, Don't Tell* transparency on the overhead projector. Read it out loud to the students with expression. Ask these questions:

❋ Do you understand what the author has written?

❋ Does it make sense?

Since these pieces are designed to show only differences in show and tell, the students will tell you that what the author has written is understandable and does make sense. Next ask:

❋ Is this piece focused?

❋ Does all the writing remain on one topic or subject?

Again, the students will answer yes. Continue by asking:

❋ Are there any examples of specific vocabulary?

❋ Which words add meaning and paint a picture in your mind?

Depending on the piece, the students will be able to find some specific vocabulary in each sample. You might underline the words they identify with colored marker.

Teacher: This author is using some great words. Now, let's look for *show, not tell.*

Ask students these questions to help them identify words, phrases, and images that show rather than tell:

- ❋ Do you feel as if you can see and hear some of the same things that Caleb experiences?

- ❋ Which images pull you into the action with Caleb? (**SAMPLE 3: 30-foot orange flames poked the night sky; counselor's whistle squealed repeated alarms; fire raced through the underbrush, close to the campground; heart pounded like dynamite; echoed somewhere deep in his head; feet sank into the ground**)

- ❋ Which images are dull and uninteresting? (**SAMPLE 2: got out of his tent, reaching high, blowing fast and hard, fire went through, Caleb was scared, he heard the words; SAMPLE 1: there was smoke, got out of his tent, saw tall, orange flames, they were scared, whistle blow really hard, that made Caleb scared, fire got bigger, it moved closer, Caleb was really, really frightened, people talking about meeting, he tried to run there**)

After examining each piece independently, ask the students which piece has the most show. Sometimes it is helpful at this point to put all of the samples on the overhead projector and compare strengths and weaknesses.

Discussion Points

If students cannot tell you why sample #3 is the strongest example of *Show, Don't Tell,* ask these questions while showing that piece on the overhead projector.

- ❋ Find a phrase that makes you feel as if you can see what is happening.

- ❋ How does the author describe Caleb's feelings?

- ❋ Are there any phrases or sentences that seem dull and distant?

Clarify Show, Don't Tell:
Tips for Teachers and Students

1. Specific, active verbs show a reader what is happening.

> **awoke, unzipped, poked, squealed and raced**

2. Exact quotes let the reader "hear" what is being said.

> **"Meet at the canoes, meet at the canoes."**

3. Showing internal reactions helps the reader "feel" the emotion of the piece.

> **Caleb's heart pounded like dynamite.**

4. Create specific images with precise vocabulary.

> **30-foot orange flames**
> **His feet sank into the ground as if they each weighed 100 pounds.**

5. Eliminate dull phrases; make each word count.

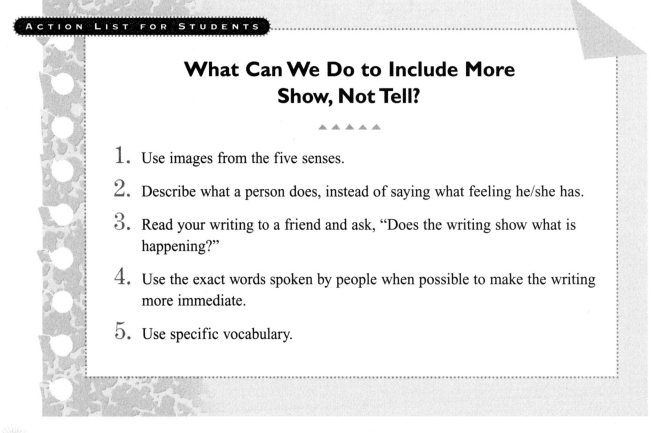

ACTION LIST FOR STUDENTS

What Can We Do to Include More Show, Not Tell?

▲ ▲ ▲ ▲ ▲

1. Use images from the five senses.

2. Describe what a person does, instead of saying what feeling he/she has.

3. Read your writing to a friend and ask, "Does the writing show what is happening?"

4. Use the exact words spoken by people when possible to make the writing more immediate.

5. Use specific vocabulary.

Fire!   ①

Caleb woke up and there was smoke. He got out of his tent and saw tall, orange flames. All of the other campers woke up, too. They were scared, Caleb could tell. All of a sudden, Caleb heard his camp counselor's whistle blow really hard. That made Caleb scared. The fire got bigger. It moved closer to the campground. Caleb was really, really frightened. His heart beat hard. He heard people talking about meeting at the canoes. He tried to run there. His feet would not go.

Fire!   ②

Caleb woke up. He smelled smoke. As he got out of his tent, he saw orange flames reaching high into the sky. The other campers woke up, too. They screamed and ran in circles. Over the noise, Caleb heard the camp counselor's whistle blowing fast and hard. The fire went through the underbrush close to the camp. Caleb was scared, real scared. His heart beat hard. He heard the words, "Meet at the canoes. Meet at the canoes." But when Caleb tried to move, his feet would not budge.

FIRE!

③

Caleb awoke to the smell of smoke. As he unzipped his tent, 30-foot orange flames poked the night sky. Surrounding campers awakened, screamed, and ran in circles. Above the din, the camp counselor's whistle squealed repeated alarms. The crackling fire raced through the underbrush, close to the campground. Caleb's heart pounded like dynamite, exploding over and over again. "Meet at the canoes, meet at the canoes," echoed somewhere deep in his head. But when Caleb tried to run, his feet sank into the ground as if they each weighed 100 pounds.

10 Writing Lessons for the Overhead   Scholastic Professional Books

Details

Is the Writing Interesting?

Details are the supporting pieces of information that help writing come alive. They can help describe a character as in Mike Emberly's book *Ruby* when he writes, *"She had run into a grimy-looking reptile whose hot breath smelled very much like dirty gym socks."* Details can help a reader visualize a setting. Tony Johnston sets the stage for her story *Alice Nizzy Nazzy* by describing the witch's home this way: *"Alice Nizzy Nazzy's* *adobe hut stood on skinny roadrunner feet. Around it grew a fence of prickly pear. Whenever she mumbled certain words to the hut (or tickled its feet), the adobe carried her over the sizzling sand…"* Details can help a reader sense what the main character is feeling or thinking. In *Bluebird Summer*, Deborah Hopkinson uses detail to show us what a granddaughter remembers of her grandmother: *"I miss watching her roll out pie crust smooth as an eggshell. And how she perched on a stool beside the tub and read us stories until our fingers pruned up."*

No one, including a child, likes to read a piece of stiff, uninteresting writing. Your students will be excited to learn that just a few carefully chosen details can add new meaning and reader-appeal to their writing. Detail does not always mean the use of adjectives; vivid verbs or specific nouns are often the best way to incorporate detail. That doesn't mean well-placed adjectives won't add meaning and interest—they can. But avoid their overuse in your examples. Instead, help your students identify short passages that add detail in the books you read to them and the books they read to themselves.

Introducing the Craft Element: Details

Begin your mini-lesson on details like this:

Teacher: Please, shut your eyes and listen to these two sentences. Try to see what I am describing.

> **Justin's glasses were crooked.**
>
> **Justin's glasses tipped to one side as if he wanted the world to be a bit out of focus.**

Which sentence did you think was more interesting? Why?

Most students will tell you that the second sentence is more interesting because of the hypothesized reason for his glasses being tilted. It gives us some insight into Justin and his personality.

Teacher: What exact words added interest to that sentence?

Students will tell you that the words *as if he wanted the world to be a bit out of focus* add the interesting perspective to that sentence.

Offer your students more practice in listening for details with these examples:

"Your recital piece needs life!" said the instructor. "Play this Grieg concerto with the same passion you use on the soccer field."	The piano teacher asked her student to play with more life.
Gwen ate her lunch quickly and hurried to find her missing mother.	Gwen swallowed her sandwich in two bites and bolted through the screen door, a photo of her missing mother clenched in her hand.
The wet earth pulled me down.	The muck grabbed my ankles and pulled me deeper into layers of ooze.
The cactus spikes dug deeper into the German Shepherd's paw with every step, forcing the dog to limp up the sidewalk and onto the porch.	The dog limped up the sidewalk and onto the porch.

Add Details and Add Meaning

▲ ▲ ▲ ▲ ▲ ▲ ▲ ▲ ▲

After you've given the students choices between dull sentences and those with details, give them the opportunity to revise. Offer students sentences that they can rewrite, adding details to make them interesting. Here are a few examples to begin:

- Jessica's sister told her to be quiet.
- The fish was on top of the water.
- Colton looked everywhere for his dog.
- The two friends made a wild pizza.

Writers look for small details that clarify setting, character, action, meaning, and conflict. Just a few details can pull a reader into the writing and keep him interested in what the author is saying.

Discussing the Craft Element: Details

Place sample #2 of the *Details* transparency on the overhead projector. Read it out loud to the students with expression. Before asking questions on details, remember to review:

※ Meaning   ※ Focus   ※ Vocabulary

Since these samples are designed to show only differences in detail, students will tell you that the piece makes sense and is focused. Underline or circle specific vocabulary with colored marker. As you might expect, there will be more specific vocabulary in a piece that contains interesting details since these two elements quite often go hand in hand. Continue the discussion by asking these questions:

※ Are there details in this writing?

※ What specific phrases or words add interest? (Avoid accepting single adjectives as a response to this question—instead, guide students into recognizing phrases like *looping it over and around.*)

Repeat the process for the other pieces, one at a time, and ask students which piece has the most details.

Students will adamantly tell you there are no interesting details in #3. They're right! They will only find a few details in sample #2 and many details in #1. Details students may identify in #1 or #2 are:

SAMPLE 1	SAMPLE 2
※ mess of bluegill, perch, or bass	※ out into Coldwater Lake in his fishing boat
※ I confessed, hoping he would take me anyway	※ how to move it up or down
※ anchored his fishing boat out in the middle of Coldwater Lake	※ waited about an hour
※ slid a pole into my hands	
※ adjust it for different depths	
※ ran the hook through the worm	
※ looping it over and around	
※ worm was in a tight ball	
※ Now no fish can steal your bait!	
※ sat in the warm sun	
※ came home with a big smile	

Encourage students to explain *how* details make writing stronger. For instance, **Next door neighbor** tells the reader that the author probably knew Mr. Dewitt fairly well. A **mess of bluegill, perch, or bass** informs the reader that Mr. Dewitt usually caught many fish and that he had taught our narrator their names, as well. **I confessed, hoping he would take me anyway** shows the reader that the author really wanted to go fishing. **Next day** tells the reader how quickly all of this happened. **Anchored his fishing boat out in the middle of Coldwater Lake** gives the reader a visual setting for the piece. **Slid a pole into my hands** paints a picture of the narrator's enthusiasm in the boat and how Mr. Dewitt began the fishing lesson. **Now no fish can steal your bait!** shows that Mr. Dewitt is experienced in these matters and the narrator has prepared her hook well. **Came home with a big smile** informs the reader that the narrator had a successful and enjoyable fishing trip with her neighbor.

Discussion Points

If the students cannot tell you that sample #1 has the most details, place that sample on the overhead projector and ask these questions:

❋ Find five details that the author uses in this piece.

❋ What do these details add to the writing?

Clarify Details: Tips for Teachers and Students

1. Small specific details describe people in a memorable way.

> **SAMPLE #1: My next door neighbor, Mr. Dewitt, always brought home a mess of bluegill, perch, or bass after one of his fishing trips.**

2. Detailed dialogue reveals character.

> **SAMPLE #1: "Are you afraid of worms?" he asked. "Nah," I said.**

3. Small details can define setting.

> **SAMPLE #1: We anchored his fishing boat out in the middle of Coldwater Lake.**

4. Specific verbs add details about how something happened.

> **SAMPLE #1: Mr. Dewitt slid a pole into my hands.**

What Can We Do to Include Details In Our Writing?

▲ ▲ ▲ ▲ ▲

1. Read one to two sentences silently to yourself and ask these questions:

   ● What did it sound, look, taste, smell, or feel like?

   ● What was the character thinking, saying, or feeling at this time?

   ● Are there any specific details that could add interest to this part?

   ● What might the character be doing physically to show his thoughts or mood?

   Then, choose one answer to add meaning to your writing.

2. Ask a friend to read your piece and ask three questions about details he would like to know. Add that information to your writing.

3. Read your draft to a friend and ask, "Is this writing interesting?"

My First Fishing Trip

①

My next door neighbor, Mr. Dewitt, always brought home a mess of bluegill, perch, or bass after one of his fishing trips. One day he asked me, "Would you like to go fishing with me tomorrow?"

"I don't know how to fish," I confessed, hoping he would take me anyway.

"It's time you learn," he said. The next day we anchored his fishing boat out in the middle of Coldwater Lake. Mr. Dewitt slid a pole into my hands. I watched as he put weights on his fishing line. He handed me the pliers and I pinched four weights onto my line. Next, he showed me how to put on the bobber and adjust it for different depths.

"Are you afraid of worms?" he asked.

"Nah," I said. So he handed me a fat, juicy nightcrawler and he took a worm for himself. He ran the hook through the worm, looping it over and around until all the worm was in a tight ball. I copied his moves the best I could.

"There," he said. "Now no fish can steal your bait!"

We sat in the warm sun all morning, but it was worth it. I came home with a big smile and five bluegills.

My Fishing Trip

2

Mr. Dewitt liked to go fishing. He was a good fisherman. One day he asked me to go fishing with him. I told him I wanted to go, but I didn't know anything about fishing. He grinned and told me that he would teach me. So, the next morning we went out into Coldwater Lake in his fishing boat. First he showed me how to put weights on my fishing line. Next, he showed me how to put the bobber on the line and how to move it up or down. My last lesson was on how to put a worm on the hook. It was gooey, but I did it. We waited about an hour and then the fish started to bite. We caught lots of bluegill that day. I'm glad Mr. Dewitt taught me how to fish.

Fishing

3

I knew a man. His name was Mr. Dewitt. He was a good friend and a good fisherman. One day he asked me if I wanted to go fishing. I wanted to go a lot. I told him I didn't know how to fish. He told me he would teach me. We went out on the lake in his boat. He showed me how to put on weights, a bobber, and a worm. We sat in the boat a long time. Then, the fish started to bite. We caught lots of fish that day. I'm glad that he took me fishing with him.

10 Writing Lessons for the Overhead   Scholastic Professional Books

Voice

Can You Hear the Author in the Writing?

Voice is the sound of the author in the writing. Voice communicates an emotion, a feeling to the reader. It's the part of the writing that truly connects writer and reader. When a piece has voice, the reader can hear the natural rhythm and syntax of the narrator's spoken language coming through the written words. I always tell students that if they can hear the human being behind the writing, then the piece has voice. I think this mini-lesson and the use of these sample pieces helps teachers and students discover voice more easily than any other strategy. Time and time again, teachers have come up to me after a classroom demonstration or mini-lesson and said, "For the first time ever I know what *writer's voice* really means."

Introducing the Craft Element: Voice

Begin your mini-lesson on voice like this:

Teacher:	Voice in writing copies, or mimics, the natural way that a person talks. If your best friend called you on the telephone and somehow disguised her voice, would you still be able to recognize her?
Students:	[Many nod their heads yes.]
Teacher:	How would you recognize your friend?
Students:	By the way she talks. By the way she stops in-between words. By the words she uses when she says something.
Teacher:	So, we can recognize certain people by the rhythm of their spoken language, or the exact words they tend to use often, or the tone or mood of their voice?
Students:	[Many nod their heads yes.]
Teacher:	Those same kinds of language patterns help readers recognize voice in writing. Please listen carefully to these sentences:

> **I am surprised. This is fun. I had no idea that you were planning a party for me.**

Tell me, do you hear true emotion in these sentences? Is this the way an excited person talks? (Answers will vary, but most students will say no.) Now, please listen carefully to these sentences:

> **I can't believe it! You really fooled me. I had no idea you were planning a party for me.**

Tell me, do you hear true emotion in these sentences? Is this the way an excited person talks?

Answers will vary, but most students will say yes to both questions.

Teacher:	Of the two groups of sentences, which one sounds the most like a real human being?

Most students will tell you that the second set sounds the most natural.

Teacher:	That's the kind of natural writer's voice we hope to have in our writing this year. The easiest way for us to find our writing voices is to write about something we deeply care about. Knowing the subject or topic and caring about it will help us use voice in our writing.

Continue your mini-lesson on voice like this:

Teacher:	Listen to these sentences and tell me something about the author:

> **My mouth dropped open. Mom and Dad were jumping off the high, high dive—something even I've never done—at the city pool. I couldn't believe my eyes.**

Some students will tell you that they know the author was amazed by what he saw because his mouth dropped open and he said he couldn't believe his eyes. Others will tell you that the author didn't expect to see his parents at the pool. Still others might tell you that the author didn't think his parents would probably ever do this—that his parents surprised him with their actions.

Teacher: Listen again, please, while I repeat the sentences:

> **My mouth dropped open. Mom and Dad were jumping off the high, high dive—something even I've never done—at the city pool. I couldn't believe my eyes.**

Does it sound like a machine, a robot, wrote these sentences? or a person?

Students will quickly tell you that a person wrote it. Then I ask, *What phrases make it sound like the natural language of a person?* Students mention phrases like:

❉ *My mouth dropped open*

❉ *Mom and Dad*

❉ *something I've never done*

❉ *I couldn't believe my eyes*

Teacher: Those are the indicators of voice. Any time you feel as if the author is speaking directly to you—sharing emotion with you—then the writing has voice. Voice brings the author, the writing, and the reader together in a tight circle of sharing.

Let It Be Their Own

▲▲▲▲▲▲▲▲▲

Since voice is born out of passion, understanding, and a deep commitment to share something with an audience on a particular topic, students need the freedom to select their writing topics and ideas. If we teachers continually provide topics for students, writing becomes an assignment. They begin to write for us, to please us, rather than to communicate. In these situations, a student's voice is lost.

Literature Look

Reading books with strong voice is a surefire way to help students understand and identify this craft element. Check these books out for some different examples of voice to read aloud:

❉ ***Freedom School, Yes!*** by Amy Littlesugar

❉ ***Dandelions*** by Eve Bunting

❉ ***Freedom Summer*** by Deborah Wiles

❉ ***The Memory Box*** by Mary Bahr

❉ ***Sister Anne's Hands*** by Marybeth Lorbiecki

❉ ***Night in the Country*** by Cynthia Rylant

Once your students can identify voice in published works, you will immediately notice an improvement in the use of voice in their writing.

Discussing the Craft Element: Voice

I have included two sets of writing samples for this important craft element. You might introduce voice with one set during your first mini-lesson. Later you can reinforce the concept by using the second set in another mini-lesson. I would not recommend using both sets on the same day; mini-lessons need to be tightly focused and relatively short.

Place sample #1 of Set A or B of the *Voice* transparencies on the overhead projector. Read it out loud to the students with expression. Before asking questions on voice, quickly review:

❋ Meaning   ❋ Focus   ❋ Vocabulary

Since these pieces are designed to only show differences in voice, students will tell you that the piece has meaning and focus. They will notice more specific vocabulary in the pieces with greater voice. I still recommend underlining or circling specific vocabulary in each piece to reinforce the power of thoughtful word choice.

Ask these questions while reading and discussing the two pieces in one of the sets, one at a time:

❋ Does this piece sound like a robot or a person wrote it?

❋ Do you think this piece has voice?

❋ Which phrases connect you to the author?

Here are some phrases that students may identify:

SET A, SAMPLE 2	SET B, SAMPLE 1
❋ my very best, all-time favorite friend	❋ some of the boys in my class tease Ernie Roberts
❋ an hour goes by like a minute	❋ They call him shortie, shrimp, and short stuff
❋ our own permanent campground	❋ It doesn't take much name-calling
❋ Keep Out Park	❋ These same boys called me Butterball Bennett
❋ with our own secret code	❋ It hurt my feelings—a lot
❋ you-go-in-and-get-the-snack, I'll-stay-here-and-watch	❋ trying to find the one that didn't make me look fat
❋ And we do!	❋ I was afraid to go to school
❋ hug the turns like an octopus on wheels	❋ "You're supposed to be so smart. Why did you get THAT grade?"
❋ that saves time	❋ I've seen the consequences of teasing
❋ best buddy—for life!	

A word of caution: indicators are just that—it's not that these words create the voice in the piece, but they are phrases that seem like natural language, that add a personality to the writing. The first set of phrases shows an enthusiasm for Jackson and the activities they do together. The overall voice is created by a combination of all words, phrasing, and rhythm—not just one or two. The second set of phrases helps create an honest voice to describe the hurt of teasing.

Sometimes students need to hear both pieces before they decide which writing has the most voice. Or, at first, they may tell you that sample #1 in Set A has voice because of the sentence *We do a lot of fun stuff.* This is a good time to ask this question: *Would a piece have voice if the reader only sees one or two examples of voice in the whole piece?* We want to show students that voice is present throughout the piece. A reader is able to hear the writer in most of the writing, not just in one isolated part. If voice refers to the natural cadence and syntax of the author's speaking language, then a reader would see and hear indicators of that voice throughout the writing.

Voice Is More Than Fun Words

▲ ▲ ▲ ▲ ▲ ▲ ▲ ▲ ▲

Young students have their own favorite vocabulary. When the new writer sees words such as *like*, *love*, or *fun* in a piece of writing, he or she immediately considers these words indicators of voice. Be patient. As you explain voice, read pieces with strong voice, and model writing with voice, the young writer will become more savvy and realize that these words alone do not constitute voice.

Discussion Points

If students cannot tell you why sample #2 in Set A and sample #1 in Set B have voice, then ask these questions:

※ Which piece sounds most like a person speaking?

※ Which piece has the most emotion?

※ Find phrases that are indicators of natural voice.

Clarify Voice: Tips for Teachers and Students

1. Language patterns similar to spoken language help create voice.

    SAMPLE: Jackson is my very best, all-time favorite friend.

2. Personal topics lend themselves to writing with a strong voice.

    SAMPLE: writing about best friends; writing about something that angers you, like teasing

3. Listing personal experience adds voice.

    SAMPLE: It hurt my feelings—a lot.

4. Writing with a sense of audience improves voice.

    SAMPLES: Late at night we send flashlight messages back and forth with our own secret code.

    I've seen the consequences of teasing, and I think it is a powerful weapon used by cowards who have no kindness or acceptance.

ACTION LIST FOR STUDENTS

What Can We Do to Include Natural Voices In Our Writing

▲ ▲ ▲ ▲ ▲

1. Select topics that are important to you—ones that you feel strongly about and know about.

2. Use words from your natural speaking vocabulary in your writing. Also use specific words that show exactly how people talk, feel, think, or act.

3. Softly say out loud what it is that you want to write as you write it.

4. After a friend reads your writing, ask him or her, "Can you hear me in this piece of writing?"

5. Read your own writing out loud and listen to its rhythm and language. Decide for yourself if your piece sounds personal.

Best Friend

(1)

My best friend is Jackson. We like being together. We do a lot of fun stuff. Sometimes we camp in the backyard. We gave our camp a special name. We both have our own tents. Late at night we send flashlight messages back and forth. We made up our own code. Two long flashes and one short flash means time for a snack. We also have bike races around the block. Jackson's sister tells us when to go. I usually win. Jackson rides fast, but he doesn't take the turns like I do. Whatever we do, we have fun. Jackson is a good buddy.

My Best Buddy

(2)

Jackson is my very best, all-time favorite friend. When we are together, an hour goes by like a minute. Jackson and I built our own permanent campground in my backyard. We call it "Keep Out Park." Our tents stay up all year in rain, sun, or snow. Late at night we send flashlight messages back and forth with our own secret code. Two long flashes and one short flash means you-go-in-and-get-the-snack, I'll-stay-here-and-watch. On Saturday mornings we have bike races around Jackson's block. His sister always starts us off by yelling, "Get on your mark, get set—GO!" And we do! I usually win. Jackson is fast, but I hug the turns like an octopus on wheels—and that saves time. Jackson is my best buddy—for life!

Teasing Is a Powerful Weapon ①

I feel that cruel teasing is always hurtful. Some of the boys in my class tease Ernie Roberts about his height. They call him *shortie*, *shrimp*, and *short stuff*. It doesn't take much name-calling before Ernie's head sinks and he refuses to answer the teacher's questions. Last year I was overweight. These same boys called me *Butterball Bennett*. It hurt my feelings—a lot. Before school, I would put on 5 to 6 different outfits trying to find the one that didn't make me look fat. I was afraid to go to school and hear what they would say. Kids at my brother's middle school make fun of him when he gets a low grade. They say, "You're supposed to be so smart. Why did you get THAT grade?" This teasing makes my brother feel self-conscious and inferior. I've seen the consequences of teasing, and I think it is a powerful weapon used by cowards who have no kindness or acceptance.

Cruel Teasing Hurts Others ②

I think cruel teasing is bad. Sometimes kids on the playground call other people names and laugh. The teased kids put their heads down and walk away. The teasing hurts their feelings. Some kids make fun of other students behind their backs. The teasers make faces at them or mimic how they walk or talk. The kids who are teased don't smile very much. My brother gets teased at the middle school if he gets a low grade. He doesn't like it either. I think teasing is cruel and should be stopped.

10 Writing Lessons for the Overhead Scholastic Professional Books

Describing Voice

What Kind of Voice Do You Hear?

One of the best ways to help young writers add voice to their writing is to present mini-lessons that attune their ears to the differences in tone or voice found in good writing. This mini-lesson guides students to identify and describe voice. Describing the author's voice simply means reading with a listening ear and naming what you hear. Does the reader hear a playful tone in the writer's voice? A reminiscent voice?

A cautionary voice? A melancholy voice? A regretful voice? An enthusiastic voice? A threatening voice? A zany or silly voice? More than one voice? Students are quickly successful at identifying the tone of the voice. In fact, after just two mini-lessons on voice, a third-grade class I visited this year was able to tell their principal that her short piece of writing had two different voices. One student explained that she began with an excited voice full of wonder when she told about seeing a doe and fawn in her backyard. But then her tone changed to a sad voice when she realized that the doe was severely injured and perhaps would not live much longer to care for her fawn.

Introducing the Craft Element: Describing Voice

Begin a mini-lesson on describing writer's voice like this:

Teacher: Does everyone always experience the same feelings while doing the same things? For instance, if all of us were to go on the fastest roller coaster in the world right now, would we all feel the same way?

Some students will announce that they would love the ride and want to do it again. Others will tell you that they would be too scared to get on. Some students might say they would go on the ride only if a good friend could accompany them.

Teacher: So, if we all rode this roller coaster and later we wrote about our experience, would all of our writing sound alike?

Students can tell you that each piece would be quite different, in both content and feeling.

Teacher: Would you all have strong feelings about your ride? How would that affect the voice in each of your pieces?

Student: My writing would be enthusiastic and joyful because I love roller coasters.

Student: My writing might be sad because I wouldn't go on the roller coaster unless someone made me.

Student: My writing might change because I've never done it—so at first I might be scared, but then if I liked it, my voice could get happy and excited, or if I didn't like it, my voice might become worried or frightened.

Teacher: That's exactly how we can describe voice. It's the feeling or the emotion that comes through with the voice. Let's look at four pieces of writing that are all about the same topic—Grandma Rose. After I read each one I'll ask you some questions and see if you can describe the writer's voice that you hear.

Discussing the Craft Element: Describing Voice

Place sample #1 of the *Describing Voice* transparencies on the overhead projector. Read it out loud to the students with expression. Before asking students to describe the voice they hear, remember to review:

- ❀ Meaning
- ❀ Focus
- ❀ Vocabulary

Since these pieces are designed to only show different kinds of voices, the students will tell you that the different pieces have meaning and focus. Students will notice more specific vocabulary in samples 1, 2, and 4 because these have writer's voice, which is conveyed through carefully chosen words. Underline or circle specific vocabulary to reinforce the power of thoughtful word choice.

Continue the discussion with these questions:

- ❀ Do you hear a human being in these words?
- ❀ Does this piece have writer's voice?
- ❀ What kind of voice do you hear? What words describe it?

Repeat the process outlined above with the other three samples.

Students will discover that they can hear the human being in the words of samples 1, 2, and 4. They will agree that these same three pieces all have a writer's voice. Their descriptions of these voices will always be the same general tone, but students may use different words to label them. For instance, several students have identified the voice in sample #1 as being a sad voice or a loving voice. But many more students have labeled it as a "remembering" voice. Remind students there are no right or wrong ways to describe voice. You can only identify the emotions and feelings you hear in the writing.

Students describe the voice in sample #2 as joyful, happy or playful. The descriptions I have heard for sample #4 are crazy, zany, fun, and silly. Sample #3 has no voice. Students usually tell me that this piece is the most poorly written sample that they have seen. The vocabulary is blah, there are no details, and it is all tell, no show.

Literature Look

Listening for the emotion in the words is exciting for students. Afterward, they take great pleasure in crafting a piece that carries a recognizable voice. If you want to listen for describable voices, read a few of these picture books to your students and decide together what voice you hear.

- ❀ *Grandmother Winter* by Phyllis Root
- ❀ *There Was an Old Lady Who Swallowed a Fly* by Simms Taback
- ❀ *The Rough-Face Girl* by Rafe Martin
- ❀ *The Memory String* by Eve Bunting
- ❀ *Flossie and the Fox* by Patricia C. McKissack
- ❀ *Be Good to Eddie Lee* by Virginia Fleming
- ❀ *The Butterfly* by Patricia Polacco

Discussion Points

If students cannot describe the voice they hear in samples 1, 2, and 4, ask these questions while looking at the sample on the overhead:

- ❋ How does the author feel about Grandmother Rose?
- ❋ What word(s) describes that feeling?
- ❋ Does the writing make you feel quiet? Happy? Silly? Sad? Angry? Thoughtful? Playful? Frustrated? Loved?

Clarify the Voice You Hear: Tips for Teachers and Students

1. Using a plan or graphic organizer in prewriting helps writers get a sense of the voice of a piece before they begin writing.

2. When an author writes about a familiar topic, his or her feelings come through in the voice. Examples:

   I never know what to expect when we are together.

   Grandmother Rose makes my face light up whenever we are together.

3. Specific details help create a distinct voice. Examples:

   Her lilac perfume wrapped around me like her warm arms.

   She always has an idea of something new we can do.

   Granny Rose tells scary, goose-bump tales from her days as a kindergarten teacher.

What Can We Do to Include A Describable Voice?

▲ ▲ ▲ ▲ ▲

1. Decide on a tone, such as excited voice, worried voice, explaining voice, wondering voice, before you begin to write. Post that voice where you can keep referring to it.

2. Remember that a piece of writing may have more than one voice. Sometimes a writer begins with one idea of what emotion is behind the writing, but as the piece develops, new feelings emerge.

3. Read your first draft to a friend and ask, "What kind of voice do you hear? Can you describe it?"

4. Put your writing away until the next day. Then, reread it out loud three different times to see if you can hear and identify your own voice in your writing.

Grandmother Rose

①

Grandmother Rose always made me feel special. Her gentle touch of my cheek showed me I was important and loved. During our long walks, she held my hand in hers and told me that my eyes sparkled with the future. When she read to me, her lilac perfume wrapped around me like her warm arms. Grandmother Rose died over five years ago and I still miss her as if she just left my house. Her memory is a friend that will live in my heart forever.

Grandmother Rose

②

Grandmother Rose makes my face light up whenever we are together. She always has an idea of something new we can do. Sometimes we bake cookies—big ones—shaped like bears with jelly tummies and raisin eyes. In the summer, we swing in the hammock under the two maple trees, while she reads book after book to me. When I spend the night at her house, we play Crazy Eight past my bedtime. Grandmother Rose is one of my best friends, even if she is 50 years older than me.

My Grandmother ③

My grandmother is a nice person. She does lots of good things with me. We bake cookies. We decorate them in fun ways. We swing in the hammock. Sometimes we just look at the trees and sometimes we read books. We play cards together on Friday nights. I like my grandmother and she likes me.

Granny Rose ④

My Granny Rose is an unusual character. I never know what to expect when we are together. Most grandmothers bake nice gingerbread cookies, but when Granny and I make cookies we call them the Blobs from the Black Lagoon. Whoever heard of a chocolate cookie with raisins, caramels, and maraschino cherries? In summer, some grandmothers take relaxing walks with their grandchildren. Not us. Granny puts on her tree-climbing helmet and boots and we climb the 30-foot red oak, scaring the black squirrels every which way. And instead of a quiet goodnight story, Granny Rose tells scary, goose-bump tales from her days as a kindergarten teacher. Boy, Granny Rose is unique, but FUN! I love her so.

Fluency

Does One Sentence Flow Into Another?

Fluency in writing refers to the natural flow of the language. We want our students' thoughts to flow from one to another smoothly and to make sense. Of course, this goal of fluency pertains to our students' reading abilities, their speech patterns, and their writing. And, really, fluency in writing is dependent on a child's language development. It will be difficult for a child to write fluently if he or she speaks in short, abrupt passages and reads word by word by word.

We as teachers can provide an environment that supports our students' growth simultaneously as speakers, listeners, readers, and writers. We can continue to read out loud to our students with expression, flowing one sentence into another. We can model fluent writing in our class demonstrations, especially when we reread what we have written as we continue to work on our drafts. We can offer many opportunities for students to read and reread their favorite stories until their own reading is smooth and fluent. As a student takes a step forward in one area, progress in others is sure to follow.

Introducing the Craft Element: Fluency

Begin your mini-lesson on fluency like this:

Teacher: Can anyone name a kind of liquid?

Students: Water. Milk. Oil. Orange Juice. Syrup.

Teacher: Yes, all of those are liquids. Liquids, and gases, are said to be fluid. When something is fluid it can flow easily from one place to another. If we tipped a plastic bottle of pancake syrup on its side, what would happen?

Students: The syrup would run out of the bottle and onto the table or floor.

Teacher: Yes, it would. We could even say that the syrup would flow, or stream out of the bottle. This year we want our ideas and words to flow, or stream, from one to another when we write. There's a special word for that skill of making words flow from one to another—it's called fluency. Fluency adds expression. It lets the natural language of the writer come through and it helps the writer's voice sing. Sometimes the kinds of sentences we use can help create fluency.

Please, listen to these sentences:

I was having fun. I was snorkeling over a coral reef. I saw exotic fish. I saw striped eels. I saw heads of coral. They were bigger than our car. I felt something. Something bit my fingertips. It happened again and again.

How did those sentences sound to you? Were they a smooth stream of words that painted a picture in your mind? Were the sentences choppy and abrupt? Was the meaning easy to follow?

Students will tell you that the sentences were short and choppy. They might even mention that several sentences began the same way. Most students will tell you that they understood what you were saying, but it wasn't fun to listen to you. Others might say they didn't get the meaning all that easily.

Teacher: Please, listen to these sentences:

> **During our vacation last winter I was able to snorkel over a coral reef. What fun! I saw exotic fish, striped eels, and coral heads larger than our car. Without warning, sharp teeth nibbled my fingertips, once, twice, and again.**

How did those sentences sound to you? Were they a steady stream of words that painted a picture in your mind? Were the sentences choppy and abrupt? Was the meaning easy to follow?

Students will tell you that these sentences were more like a steady stream of words that painted a picture. They will also tell you that the meaning was much easier to follow. When you ask them *why*, their responses will vary. Keep speaking with them about meaning, vocabulary, and sentence structure. Ask them if many of these sentences started the same way, as in the last group. Reread both sets again if your class needs extra support. Ask them which set had ideas or sentences that flowed from one into another.

Teacher: When we speak we use all kinds of sentences to make meaning. We use short sentences, long sentences, quotes, questions, sentences with short phrases, sentences with long phrases, compound sentences and interjections. When we make meaning we use all the sentence tools we have to say it just right. This year in our writing we want to use different kinds of sentences to make meaning. We want our words, sentences, and ideas to flow from one to the next. As you become more fluent writers, you will think more about how the words and sentences sound as they make meaning. Let's look at two pieces of writing that are on the same topic. I think you'll find that one is written more fluently than the other.

Discussing the Craft Element: Fluency

Place sample #1 of the *Fluency* transparency on the overhead projector. Read it out loud to the students with expression. Before asking questions on fluency, remember to review:

- Meaning
- Focus
- Vocabulary

Since these pieces are designed to only show differences in fluency, the students will tell you that the author has conveyed meaning and focus. The students will notice specific vocabulary. Be sure to underline or circle these words, which helps students remember some of this vocabulary when they are searching for specific words as they write.

Continue with these questions:

* Does every sentence flow easily into the next?

* Could you hear the natural flow of spoken language?

* Were there any places where the writing sounded chopped off, or abrupt?

Repeat the process outlined above for the other piece. Afterward, it is sometimes helpful to look at both pieces simultaneously on the overhead projector to compare and contrast. Now ask: *Which piece is more fluent?* Below are comments typical of those I have received from students about these pieces:

* In sample #1, students will tell you that the ideas flow fairly well, but not the language. Many sentences begin with *it* or *I*—that pattern creates an abruptness that breaks up fluency.

* In sample #2, students will notice that the sentences flow much more smoothly. The language keeps the reader moving faster and faster through the scene.

* It is difficult to hear any natural flow of language in sample #1. This is not how people think or speak; therefore it sounds unnatural when reading this piece.

* In sample #2, the natural flow carries the reader through the writing with ease.

* Students will mention many places in sample #1 where the writing sounds chopped or abrupt. It's almost as if this writer was trying to use only four- to six-word sentences, like an exercise. Help the students note how many abbreviated sentences are in this piece of writing. Perhaps highlight them with colored marker. It will be more difficult for students to find abrupt language in sample #2.

Students will announce that sample #2 is definitely more fluent. Their reasons for their choice will vary. Some explanations may include:

1. The different kinds of sentences help tie the meaning together.

2. Some sentences begin with phrases, some directly with the subject.

3. Some sentences were longer to explain things and some sentences were short, but the blend works.

4. It seems as if each sentence in sample #2 starts where the one before it left off.

5. Sample #2 sounds like a person telling another person how it happened.

Discussion Points

If students cannot tell you why sample #2 is more fluent, ask these questions:

- ❋ Is this piece easy to read and understand?
- ❋ Does the writer use different kinds and lengths of sentences?
- ❋ Do the words and ideas flow from one to another like when a person tells a story?
- ❋ Can you find sentences that combine two or more ideas?

Clarify Fluency: Tips for Teachers and Students

1. Creating a brief plan during prewriting helps writers sequence ideas so that they flow logically from one to another in the writing.

2. A combination of different kinds of sentences—simple, compound, and complex—forms the natural cadence of spoken and written language. For instance:

   Yeow, I thought, I don't want to see this anymore. I shut my eyes—tight—for several seconds and wished that it would float away. But as I slowly opened my eyelids, I could see the shadow sliding closer and closer to my bed.

3. Transitions, both words and phrases, carry one thought into another:

   But I guess I scared the shadow away because this morning it was nowhere in sight.

What Can We Do to Make Our Writing More Fluent?

▲ ▲ ▲ ▲ ▲

1. Read your writing out loud and see if it has the same natural rhythm as spoken lanugage.

2. After a friend reads your draft, ask, "Does each sentence flow into the next?"

3. Try to avoid the use of just one kind of sentence over and over again.

4. Practice telling a friend what you are going to write beforehand. Listen to yourself talk, paying attention to the words and expressions you choose, and then try to write the same way you would speak.

Late Night Visitor

I woke up. It was the middle of the night. Something moved in my room.
It was a large shadow. It was big and looked like it had arms. It moved
from one side to another. What was making the shadow? I couldn't see
anything. I closed my eyes. I wished it away. They were shut real tight.
Then I opened my eyes. The shadow was still in my room. It came closer
to me. I shouted. I tried to scare it away. I made a lot of noise. It didn't
go anywhere. I decided to stay awake. I would wait until the shadow
went away. I kept staring and staring at it for a long time. It finally went
away. This morning the shadow was gone.

Late Night Visitor ②

I awoke in the middle of the night and saw a slippery, black shadow
skating across my room. It appeared to have arms that reached out for
me. *YEOW*, I thought, *I don't want to see this anymore.* I shut my eyes—
tight—for several seconds and wished that it would float away. But as I
slowly opened my eyelids, I could see the shadow sliding closer and
closer to my bed. "Get out of here, you monster!" I shouted. For a
second I thought it had disappeared. But I was wrong. It slipped behind
my bed and danced on the wall. "Okay, Buster," I announced. "I can be
just as stubborn as you!" For the rest of the night I never let the visitor
out of my sight. But I guess I scared the shadow away because this
morning it was nowhere in sight. "Ha! Gotcha!"

10 Writing Lessons for the Overhead   Scholastic Professional Books

Dialogue

Who's Saying What?

Dialogue is the transcription of a conversation between two or more people. It captures the actual words spoken; these are set off from the rest of the text by quotation marks. Dialogue can reveal character, add life or voice to writing, and move the plot forward. Young writers love to use dialogue in their stories. But we must remember to be patient—it takes quite a bit of experimentation before they use it well. Students also need some basic instruction about dialogue. They need to know that:

1. Tags are necessary to identify speakers (*he said, Mom repeated, asked Tom*).

2. Simple tags are preferred so they do not detract from the dialogue.

3. Dialogue and narrative work together to create a scene.

4. Writers begin a new paragraph every time the speaker changes.

Avoid Flowery Tags

While examining dialogue in published books, help students discover that most tags are simple and unobtrusive. Tags are used to identify speakers, not to steal the show. Writers only occasionally use more elaborate tags, such as *stated, yelled, announced,* or *mumbled*. In most cases the word *said* is the tag of choice. Let the conversation reveal action and emotion while the tags become quiet bystanders.

Introducing the Craft Element: Dialogue

Begin a mini-lesson on dialogue like this:

Teacher: Why do people talk to one another?

Students' responses will vary. Some will say they talk to pass on information. Others will say they talk to explain how to do something. Some students will say the reason people talk is to get to know one another or to share stories. You'll probably hear about 10 different reasons for conversation.

Teacher: When we write, it's fun to capture the exact words people say to one another. These conversations are called dialogue. Dialogue can help our readers get to know a character, it can provide information, it can keep the narrative moving, or add *show, not tell*. But just like anything else in writing, it helps if we think about how we want to write dialogue. All by itself, it can sometimes sound unnatural. Please, listen to this bit of dialogue:

> **"You should have seen it!" she said.**
>
> **"What?" she asked.**
>
> **"This beautiful creature!"**
>
> **"Describe it for me," she said.**
>
> **"The top was a bubble of purple. Beneath that there were about twenty blue tentacles."**
>
> **"Sounds exciting!" she said.**
>
> **"It was!"**

Can you tell me who is talking and what they are talking about?

Students will tell you that they are confused. There are no names, no setting, no context for this dialogue.

Teacher: Please, listen carefully again. This time I will add a little narrative to the dialogue:

> **Jaime ran out of the sea and pulled off her mask and snorkel.**
>
> **"You should have seen the jellyfish that I just saw," she said, pointing toward the water.**
>
> **"What was it like?" her mom asked.**
>
> **"The bell was like a bubble of purple," explained Jaime. "And about twenty blue tentacles hung beneath it, swaying in the water!"**
>
> **"Sounds exciting," said her mom. "Do you think we could find it together?"**
>
> **"Let's try," said Jaime, and she followed her mom into the sea.**

Now can you tell me who was talking and what they were talking about?

Students will be able to describe the conversation in detail.

Teacher: This year we want to make sure that our dialogues are understandable and add meaning to our writing. I have two sample pieces of dialogue. Help me decide which could add meaning to a piece of writing.

Discussing the Craft Element: Dialogue

Place sample #1 of Set A or B of the *Dialogue* transparencies on the overhead projector. Read it out loud to the students with expression. (Since we are looking at chunks of dialogue out of context, I do not use the questions about meaning, focus, and vocabulary.) Ask these questions:

- ❋ Do you understand who is speaking each time?

- ❋ Do you understand what is being said?

- ❋ Could this dialogue add information or interest to a piece of writing?

- ❋ Is there a blend of dialogue and narration?

Repeat the above questions with the other piece from the same set. Then ask the students which selection is stronger dialogue and why.

NOTE: Only use one set of samples during your first mini-lesson on dialogue. Save the other set for use at a later time. Our goal is to keep each mini-lesson focused and fairly brief.

Set A

Students will readily tell you that sample #2 is the stronger piece. These are some of the reasons they may cite:

- ❋ In sample #1, the reader knows who is saying what at the beginning. The first half is tagged, but the second half is not. Students could go back and determine who is saying what. But would a reader want to take time to do that?

- ❋ Sample #2 is clearly tagged from beginning to end. The fifth line is not tagged, but because of content and placement we know that Brandon said this.

- ❋ Sample #2 states quite clearly what has been said by both brother and sister.

- ❋ In sample #1, the beginning is understandable. After that we recognize the words, but they don't carry much information or interest. It is just idle bickering that would not move the writing forward. This long list of *he saids, she saids* becomes tedious to a reader and distracts him from the focus of the writing.

- ❋ The dialogue in sample #2 adds information about the setting for Brandon and Marie's disagreement. We know exactly why Brandon is angry with Marie. We know that Marie wants to prove herself innocent.

* In sample #1, all we know is that Brandon tells Marie that he wants her cat to come face to face with his dog. We have no idea why he is angry, where they are at this time, what Marie is going to do to keep this from happening. The dialogue in sample #1 could be eliminated from the writing without removing any important information.

* Mixing the short narrative descriptions into the dialogue in sample #2 provides setting, more personality of the two characters, and an exit for both characters to move into the next scene.

* Sample #1 only offers dialogue, no narrative, which makes the writing dry and lifeless.

Set B

Students will say sample #2 is the stronger. These are some of the reasons they may cite:

* Sample #1 of Set B is not even true dialogue. (But this is exactly what many students begin writing when trying to add dialogue to their pieces.) We do know who said what to whom but it is written as tell—as straight narrative.

* In sample #2 of Set B we have clear tags and the quotation marks separate the exact words spoken by Antonio and Luke.

* In sample #1, we get the gist of what was said. We do not see the exact words.

* Sample #2 provides the exact words spoken by Antonio and Luke. We read a natural conversation between two friends.

* Sample #1 does add some information about what took place, but again, it is dull, lifeless, and does not add interest.

* Sample #2 does add interest because we get a sense of what each boy values at the fair. We learn about Antonio and Luke's personalities. We know that Antonio can be persuasive.

* In sample #1, there is no blend of dialogue and narrative, only straight narrative.

* In sample #2, the blend of narrative and dialogue offers the reader what is said, plus expressions, setting, and action.

Discussion Points

If students cannot tell you that sample #2 in Set A and sample #2 in Set B use dialogue more effectively, ask these questions:

※ Can you tell where this dialogue is being spoken?

※ Are quotation marks used around the words spoken?

※ Can you easily identify who is speaking each time?

※ Could this excerpt add meaning to a piece of writing?

Clarify Dialogue: Tips for Teachers and Students

1. Small bits of narration can provide setting for the dialogue.

> **"You keep that mangy dog of yours away from my Fluffy!" yelled Marie, shutting her bedroom door tightly.**

> **As the boys hurried to the fairground, they debated about what to see first.**

2. Clear tags help readers easily identify speakers.

> **"Before you threaten me again, don't you think you should check your facts?" asked Marie. "Let's visit the scene of the crime."**

> **"Fine," barked Brandon. "Then you won't be able to squirm out of it."**

3. What is spoken can reveal character and emotion.

> **"I told you to leave my stuff alone," he called through the door, "but noooooo, you had to go and ride my bike!"**

What Can We Do to Write Strong Dialogue?

▲ ▲ ▲ ▲ ▲

1. Use tags that clearly identify speakers.

2. Blend dialogue and narrative to show more of the scene.

3. Give your writing to a friend and ask, "Can you tell who is saying what?"

4. Include some new information about a character, setting, or action to add interest to your dialogues.

Fluffy Meets Godzilla

①

"Time for Fluffy to meet Godzilla," said Brandon.

"Keep your dog away from my cat," said Marie.

"Make me!"

"I will!" she said.

"Oh, yeah?" he said.

"Yeah!" she said.

"Big talk," he said.

"You bet!" she said.

"You messed with my stuff," he said.

"Did not!"

"Uh-huh!"

"Did not!"

"Did, too!"

"I'll show you."

"Okay."

10 Writing Lessons for the Overhead   Scholastic Professional Books

Fluffy Meets Godzilla

②

"It's time Fluffy meets Godzilla," said Brandon, with a bit of brotherly sneer.

"You keep that mangy dog of yours away from my Fluffy!" yelled Marie, shutting her bedroom door tightly.

"I told you to leave my stuff alone," he called through the door, "but · noooooo, you had to go and ride my bike!"

"I didn't ride your bike," said Marie, through the keyhole. "I don't even like your bike."

"Then you rode it just to get my goat! So now, your cat gets my dog!"

"Before you threaten me again, don't you think you should check your facts?" asked Marie. "Let's visit the scene of the crime."

"Fine," barked Brandon. "Then you won't be able to squirm out of it!"

Fair Night

①

Antonio told Luke that the fair had opened in town. Luke said he wanted to go right away. Antonio said he did, too. Antonio asked Luke what he wanted to see first. Luke said he wanted to walk through the haunted pyramid. Antonio said no. He said that would be too crowded since everyone in town was looking forward to it. He said that they should try the Ferris wheel first. Luke said he didn't know whether he'd like the Ferris wheel or not. He said that he'd never been on one. Antonio said it would be fun and he should try it. Luke said okay. He'd give it a try.

Fair Night

②

"Hey, Luke!" hollered Antonio. "Did you know that the fair is open?"

Luke's face got as bright as a new silver dollar. "I've been waiting for it to come to town," he said. "Let's go right now."

"You bet!" answered Antonio.

As the boys hurried to the fairground, they debated about what to see first. "Let's see the haunted pyramid that everyone's been talking about," said Luke. "It sounds scary enough to make your hair fall out."

"Nah," said Antonio. "Everybody and their brother will start there. Let's try the Ferris wheel. We can be the first ones to see across town tonight."

"You're not going to believe this," said Luke. "But I've never been on a Ferris wheel before. I'm not sure how I feel about swinging up that high."

"You'll love it, man," said Antonio, putting his arm around Luke. "It's the closest thing to flying you'll ever know. Give it a try. And if you don't like it, we'll holler at the guy to let us off."

Luke smiled wide. "Flying huh?" he said. "Okay, I'll give it a try. Let's go!"

Leads

Do You Want to Read On?

Leads are the first words an audience reads. A lead is an invitation to readers, a lure to entice them to become involved and read more. The good news is that there are many ways to write strong leads and apprentice writers can learn by reading, listening, and thoughtfully studying examples. As teachers, we need to create an atmosphere of experimentation.

Encourage students to try different kinds of leads for a piece and see which one works best. Find different leads in picture books, novels, or newspaper articles, and discuss them with your class. Ask them:

✻ What do you notice about this lead?

✻ How does it make you feel?

✻ Do you want to read on?

Post a few published leads in the room as examples of dramatic, question, dialogue, reflection, contrast, introduction, or action leads.

But even as you discuss and study leads, don't cripple your students by placing so much importance on their first few words that they struggle and sit and fret before putting pencil to paper. The easiest way to polish a lead is *after* the first draft is written. Don't squelch the passion or the commitment that students have in their writing. Let them write what's on their minds and in their hearts. Revision is the time to go back and rework leads. At that time writers know the intent and voice of their pieces. They can rewrite their leads to set the stage for the rest of the piece. (But don't be surprised when some of your students craft strong leads in the first draft. Many writers have an uncanny instinct to begin with honest, poignant leads that knock our socks off!)

Introducing the Craft Element: Leads

Begin your mini-lesson on leads like this:

Teacher: How many of you have ever gone fishing?

A few students will raise their hands.

Teacher: When you go fishing, what do you use to attract a fish to your fishing line?

Some students will say worms, others will say crickets. Some will say cheese, and yet others will say lures.

Teacher: Why do you use those particular things to attract the fish to the line?

Students will say that these are the kinds of things fish like to eat. Even lures are made to look like the food that fish like. You need to use the best bait to bring them to the hook.

Teacher: Authors want to attract readers to their writing. So, they try to use the best language, the kind of words and meaning that readers like. And

Literature Look

These books offer a variety of leads:

✻ **The Best Place** by Susan Meddaugh

✻ **Click, Clack, Moo, Cows That Type** by Doreen Cronin

✻ **Joey Pigza Swallowed the Key** by Jack Gantos

✻ **Journey** by Patricia MacLachlan

✻ **The Library** by Sarah Stewart

✻ **When Vera Was Sick** by Vera Rosenberry

since leads are the words that begin our pieces, we want them to act like bait, or lures. We want to attract readers so they continue to read everything we have written. Please, listen carefully to these two leads:

Abby felt sad. Today was the day her best friend was moving away.

Abby shut her bedroom door and crawled back into bed. Maybe, just maybe, if she didn't leave her room, time would stop. And if time stopped, then her best friend Marcie would not move away—today or ever.

Which lead grabbed you the most?

Most students will tell you that they liked the second lead better. When asked why, they share that it really shows how much Abby likes her friend Marcie and how she'll try anything—even stopping time—to get her to stay. In other words, the lead involves the reader with Abby's feelings on a much deeper level than the first lead. There is more characterization of Abby in lead #2. Abby seems like a real person who we can see after hearing the second lead.

Teacher: That's what good leads do. They set the stage. They introduce us to character, setting, or the problem in a sincere way that makes us want to know more.

Discussing the Craft Element: Leads

Place sample #1 of Set A, B, C, D, or E from the *Leads* transparencies on the overhead projector. Since we are just working with the first few words of a piece, do not ask questions about meaning, focus, or vocabulary. Before you ask questions of the students, give them an opportunity to assess how strong they think the lead is.

Teacher: I'm going to read this lead two times. Please, listen carefully. On a scale of one to ten—ten being the best lead you've ever read in your entire life and one being the most boring, uninviting lead you've ever read—decide what score you would give this example.

After you read the lead, ask four to six students to share their scores. After each student announces her score, ask her why she rated it as she did.
Then ask the class these questions:

❋ Does this lead make you want to read on?

❋ What kind of a lead would you say this is? Dramatic? Contrast? Introduction? Question? Grabber? Reflective? Dialogue? Describe the lead the best you can.

❋ Would you be interested in using this kind of lead in your own writing sometime?

Repeat the process outlined above with the other one or two leads in that same set. Of course, answers will vary, but you will see consistency in the leads that students like. Remember though—students are honest. They will see a need to identify the leads they feel are weak and inadequate. Their scores of one and two will be one indication. Or they might compose a name for these weak leads, but usually students just want to tell you that they are boring. This is fine, because anything they consider boring is usually something they avoid in their future writing.

Student reactions to the pieces are likely to include the following:

❋ In Set A, most students will consider #3 the strongest lead.

❋ They will describe it as a *grabber*. You will definitely see an increase in the number of leads that will begin with an onomatopoeic word, or an interjection. Students like the liveliness of that type of lead.

❋ In Set B, you might have a split between students favoring #1 and #2. Students will tell you that #3 is boring. Students will describe #1 as fantasy or something out of the ordinary that makes us stretch our imagination. It makes them laugh to picture it in their minds. But it has a great contrast when old man Thurber suggests this isn't anything out of the ordinary.

❋ Students identify #2 in Set B as a dialogue lead and they like the way it shows old man Thurber's personality. He takes the worms for granted while Billy is in awe.

❋ Both #1 and #2 in Set B would entice someone to read on.

❋ For Set C, it depends on the sophistication of the reader/writer when choosing between #2 and #3. Students that like the use of opening words like *pump, pump, flutter* will enthusiastically support it as the strongest. They consider this an action lead.

❋ The students that prefer #3 in Set C may be readers of longer books that like a slower, more reflective lead. They like the way this lead lures the audience to read on. I have seen many students begin using this kind of lead after studying its form.

❋ Almost all students will give #1 in Set D a high score. They recognize the contrast immediately and think this is a strong way to lead a reader into a piece of writing. The words *but after what happened today* are a great teaser. Students want to know what it was that happened. Again, after students see and discuss this type of lead, they begin to incorporate similar leads into their own writing.

❊ Students will prefer sample #2 in Set E. This lead has an unwritten promise that an event is either going to prevent G.B.'s successful start to the race, or present a challenge early into the race. Students will mention that the vocabulary *shifted* and *vaulting* add strength to this lead. The narrow window of time is an easy device for students to learn to include in their leads in the future. It adds a sense of urgency.

NOTE: In one mini-lesson I would suggest using only two sets of leads. Save the other sets for a refresher mini-lesson, or as a catapult into revision on leads.

Clarify Leads: Tips for Teachers and Students

1. Leads that use specific, active verbs engage readers immediately.

> **Zoom! Jacob's roller coaster car streaked ahead until the electricity failed and trapped him inside Dead Man's Tunnel.**

2. Contrast leads entice readers to wonder about the cause for a change.

> **Most days a sandwich and apple make a great lunch, but after what happened today I opened the refrigerator and gobbled everything in sight!**

3. Strong leads set the tone for the rest of the piece.

> **G.B.'s eyes shifted from dog to dog. In less than a minute, he and his team would be vaulting across the frozen North.**

4. Dialogue leads introduce character personalities.

> **"What's that?" yelled Billy McGee, as he pointed to the floor.**
> **"The worms!" said old man Thurber, shaking his head. "It happens every year on the first day of spring. A hundred of 'em—go ahead count—march in here on their tails."**
> **"Why?" asked Billy.**
> **"Nobody knows," said old man Thurber. "But it's near impossible to sell any bait after the customers see 'em."**

What Can We Do to Improve Our Leads?

▲ ▲ ▲ ▲ ▲

1. Take time to study different kinds of leads in published writing.

2. During revision, write two to four different leads and see which one your friends think is stronger.

3. Use specific vocabulary in leads.

4. Read your lead to a friend and ask, "Do you want to hear more?"

SET A   Jacob was riding in a fast roller coaster car. It zoomed ahead and went into a tunnel where it stopped. ①

Jacob's roller coaster car zoomed into Dead Man's Tunnel just as the electricity failed. ②

Zoom! Jacob's roller coaster car streaked ahead until the electricity failed and trapped him inside Dead Man's Tunnel. ③

SET B   One hundred earthworms stood on their tails and marched into Lou's bait shop on the first day of spring. "Not again," shouted old man Thurber. ①

"What's that?" yelled Billy McGee, as he pointed to the floor. ②

"The worms!" said old man Thurber, shaking his head. "It happens every year on the first day of spring. A hundred of 'em—go ahead count—march in here on their tails."

"Why?" asked Billy.

"Nobody knows," said old man Thurber. "But it's near impossible to sell any bait after the customers see 'em."

Some worms stood on their tails and went into the bait store. Old man Thurber yelled that this wasn't the first time this had happened. ③

10 Writing Lessons for the Overhead   Scholastic Professional Books

SET C　　A butterfly dried its wings. Evan watched. He was amazed by what he saw.

Pump! Pump! Flutter! Evan's mouth opened wide as the young butterfly spread its wings and flew over his head.

Most days we all take nature for granted. That is unless we're lucky enough to witness something amazing—something that grabs us by the throat and won't let go. That's exactly what happened to my friend Evan.

SET D　　Most days a sandwich and apple make a great lunch, but after what happened today I opened the refrigerator and gobbled everything in sight!

I usually eat a sandwich and apple every day for lunch. Today was different. Today I ate all the food in the refrigerator!

SET E　　There he was—the musher, and his dogs. He looked over his team one last time. The race was going to start.

G.B.'s eyes shifted from dog to dog. In less than a minute, he and his team would be vaulting across the frozen North.

Children's Books Cited

Bahr, Mary. *The Memory Box*. Chicago: Albert Whitman, 1995.

Bunting, Eve. *Dandelions*. San Diego: Harcourt, Inc., 1995.

———. *Flower Garden*. San Diego: Harcourt Brace and Company, 1994.

———. *The Memory String*. New York: Clarion Books, 2000.

———. *Rudi's Pond*. New York: Clarion Books, 1999.

Cronin, Doreen. *Click, Clack, Moo, Cows That Type*. New York: Simon & Schuster Books for Young Readers, 2000.

Emberly, Michael. *Ruby*. Boston: Little, Brown and Company, 1990.

Fleming, Virginia. *Be Good to Eddie Lee*. New York: Philomel Books, 1993.

Gantos, Jack. *Joey Pigza Swallowed the Key*. New York: Farrar Straus Giroux, 1998.

Hopkinson, Deborah. *Bluebird Summer*. New York: Greenwillow Books, 2001.

Johnston, Tony. *Alice Nizzy Nazzy*. New York: G.P. Putnam's Sons, 1995.

Kasza, Keiko. *Don't Laugh, Joe!* New York: G.P. Putnam's Sons, 1997.

Littlesugar, Amy. *Freedom School, Yes!* New York: Philomel Books, 2001.

Lorbiecki, Marybeth. *Sister Anne's Hands*. New York: Dial Books for Young Readers, 1998.

MacLachlan, Patricia. *Journey*. New York: Delacorte Press, 1991.

Martin, Rafe. *The Rough-Face Girl*. New York: G.P. Putnam's Sons, 1992.

McKissack, Patricia C. *Flossie and the Fox*. New York: Dial Books, 1986.

McPhail, David. *Mole Music*. New York: Henry Holt and Company, 1999.

Meddaugh, Susan. *The Best Place*. Boston: Houghton Mifflin Company, 1999.

Polacco, Patricia. *The Butterfly*. New York: Philomel Books, 2000.

Root, Phyllis. *Grandmother Winter*. Boston: Houghton Mifflin Company, 1999.

Rosenberry, Vera. *When Vera Was Sick*. New York: Henry Holt and Company, 1998.

Rylant, Cynthia. *Night in the Country*. New York: Simon & Schuster, 1986.

Schaefer, Lola. *This Is the Sunflower*. New York: Greenwillow Books, 2000.

Stewart, Sarah. *The Library*. New York: Farrar Straus Giroux, 1995.

Taback, Simms. *There Was an Old Lady Who Swallowed a Fly*. New York: Viking, 1997.

Wiles, Deborah. *Freedom Summer*. New York: Atheneum Books for Young Readers, 2001.